DESIGNING A WOMAN'S LIFE

A Bible Study and Workbook

JUDITH COUCHMAN

MULTNOMAH BOOKS

SISTERS, OREGON

DESIGNING A WOMAN'S LIFE
BIBLE STUDY AND WORKBOOK

A Practical Guide to Discovering Your Unique Purpose and Passion

published by Multnomah Publishers, Inc.

© 1996 by Judy C. Couchman

International Standard Book Number: 0–88070–887–5

Cover photo by Jim Vecchione
Printed in the United States of America

Most Scripture quotations are from:
The Holy Bible, New International Version (NIV)
© 1973, 1984 by International Bible Society,
used by permission of Zondervan Publishing House

Also quoted:
The King James Version (KJV)

FOR INFORMATION:
MULTNOMAH PUBLISHERS, INC., PO BOX 1720, SISTERS, OREGON 97759

Library of Congress Cataloging-in-Publication Data
Couchman, Judith, 1953-
    Designing a woman's life:a Bible study and workbook/Judith Couchman.
        p.   cm.   Includes bibliographical references.
    ISBN 0-88070-887-5 (alk. paper)
    1. Woman (Christian theology)—Study and teaching. 2. Women—Religious
life—Study and teaching. 3. Spiritual life—Christianity—Study and teaching.
I. Title.
BT704.C679   1996   96-28011
248.8'43—dc20   CIP
                00 01 02 03 04 — 10 9 8 7 6

For Ana, Beth, Claudia, Deena —

forever friends who brought Clarity into my life

with purpose and passion.

BY JUDITH COUCHMAN

Designing a Woman's Life
Loving God with All Your Heart
A Very Present Help
Shaping a Woman's Soul
Lord, Have You Forgotten Me?
Lord, Please Help Me to Change
Why Is Her Life Better Than Mine?
If I'm So Good, Why Don't I Act That Way?
Getting a Grip on Guilt

Contents

Many thanks to Questar/Multnomah for not only publishing my book *Designing a Woman's Life* but also believing a companion Bible study would enhance its mission. I especially thank Carol Bartley and Rebecca Price for adopting me into their publishing family.

My deep gratitude also extends to that book's readers for calling, writing, or talking face to face about how you needed its message, how it clarified your spiritual journey, and what you're pursuing now because of its influence. Changed lives are an author's delight.

I am also grateful for the research assistance of my niece Melissa Honeywell, and, as always, I'm indebted to my prayer team. Along with my mother, Opal Couchman, her friend Mae Lammers, and my sister Shirley Honeywell, these women prayed for this study's influence: Charette Barta, Win Couchman, Madalene Harris, Karen Hilt, and Nancy Lemons.

May you feel their prayers and the Holy Spirit's presence as you study the Scriptures and ponder your life's purpose.

Reflection

Designing a Life Worth Living

*I began these pages for myself, in order to think out my own
particular pattern of living, my own individual balance of life,
work and human relationships. And since I think best with
a pencil in my hand, I started naturally to write.*

ANNE MORROW LINDBERGH

"God never wastes anything in your life."

A friend told me this years ago, and at the time I resented her for it. Bogged down by pain, I couldn't fathom how God would use my disappointing circumstances and my thrashing about for mission and meaning, for anything. And certainly not for anything good in other women's lives.

I wish I had known then what I know now. A philosopher once explained, "Life can only be understood backwards; but it must be lived forwards."[1] How true. Often the hindsight of the years, or even the generations, casts the light of understanding.

I stepped into that light last year while creating the book *Designing a Woman's Life*. As Anne Morrow Lindbergh did decades ago, I began those pages to think through my pattern of living, the intensity of almost two decades, and what God had taught me about purpose and passion.

While experiencing those years, I saw no emerging pattern at all. But halfway through the soul-searching act of book writing, I realized I'd been viewing my life's tapestry from the wrong side. I'd been focusing on the fabric's underbelly, full of knots and loose ends and piercing stabs. I needed to flip over the fabric to admire the smooth, tightly woven, surprising design on the reverse side.

Observing from that viewpoint, I discerned a definite, remarkably beautiful pattern. And even more surprising, that pattern — the principles God taught me and the faith they produced — now helps other women discover their own unique design and purpose in life. Certainly my mourning had turned into dancing.

But while the book provided a broad philosophical base, I felt it needed a practical guidebook to prompt women toward weaving God's eternal principles into their everyday lives. You're holding that guidebook, a Bible study, in your hands.

EXPLORING THIS STUDY

If you haven't read the book *Designing a Woman's Life*, don't be hesitant to pursue this Bible study. Although the book serves as a complement to the study, you can plunge into these sessions without having read it. However, if you want to read the book and gain a fuller understanding of the pursuit of purpose, it is available through your local Christian bookstore.

In addition to "standing on its own," this guidebook provides the flexibility to study individually, with a partner, or as a group. Whatever setting you choose, don't let a session's length discourage you from working through it. If your time is limited, try one or more of these options.

• Divide each session into two lessons, turning the study into sixteen short blocks that better fit your schedule.

• Divide each session into as many short "bites" as you need.

• Look up only the Bible verses with an asterisk (*) after them. They are most crucial to understanding the Scriptures and completing an answer. To study more in depth, review all of the verses in a question.

• Answer only the personal questions you deem most important for your progress and remembrance.

• Skip the optional activities.

• If you're part of a group, complete the study together during a session, rather than ahead of time.

Searching for purpose requires time and commitment, but the process isn't confined to eight lessons in eight weeks. Hopefully, these sessions will plant perennial seeds that will blossom, bit by bit, over your lifetime.

LISTENING TO THE SPIRIT

However you approach this Bible study, its ideas and principles captivate the heart only if you're open to the Holy Spirit's assistance. He is the one — not words on paper or ideas flung at our ears — who whispers God's desires deep within the soul. He is, and ever will be, the one to trust for guidance. I hope that more than anything you will follow his lead not only while pursuing your purpose, but for the rest of your days.

For this is how to design a meaningful life, a life worth living.

Significance

Embracing Our Innate Worth

✾

To me, one of the proofs that God's hand is behind
and all throughout this marvelous Book we know as the Bible
is the way it continually touches upon this very fear in us —
the fear that we are so insignificant as to be forgotten.
That we are nothing.
Unconsciously, His Word meets this fear,
and answers it.

AMY CARMICHAEL

A SIMPLE TRUTH

You are deeply significant because God created you.

WORDS TO REMEMBER

"How great is the love the Father has lavished on us." — 1 John 3:1

HIS LOVE, OUR SIGNIFICANCE

My mother still beams when she repeats this story from my oldest sister's childhood. It varies a bit with each telling, but the message remains constant. Whenever Shirley returned home from kindergarten or another outing without Mom, she marched into the house and yelled, "I'm here!" This announcement signaled my mother's part in the routine: She fawned over her daughter's presence.

Mom had no trouble with her role in the performance. This young child issued from her blood; this Shirley Temple look-alike sprang from her loving procreation. How could she not delight in her daughter's existence? Any other response would have been utterly unthinkable. Nearly fifty years later Mother still feels this joy in regard to her children and grandchildren. Though she encourages and revels in our accomplishments, more than anything Mom loves us just because we belong to her.

This, too, is the way of God the Father. He declares to his children, "I have loved you with an everlasting love" (Jeremiah 31:3). He draws us to himself for the sheer pleasure of it. He loves us not for who we are, or what we do, or who we can or will be. He loves us because he created us, because we belong to him.

It is a profoundly simple reality.

FIRST THOUGHTS

1. What is your initial, not-thinking-about-it response to the statement, "You are deeply significant because God created you?"

you are special no matter what, not because you are pretty or smart or built to A T but because God made you.

2. Do you *really believe* you are significant? Why, or why not? How is this evident in your life?

A CLOSER LOOK AT SCRIPTURE

3. We can begin to grasp God's profound love for us by studying what the Scriptures say. Look up the following verses and in the provided spaces, describe his love for us. Even if you're familiar with a verse, take time to filter its meaning through your soul.

A reminder: Throughout this study, you may choose to look up only the verses with an asterisk (*) if your time is limited.

- Lamentations 3:22–23

- Romans 8:35–39*

- Ephesians 3:16–19*

WHAT HE DID FOR LOVE

4. Fortunately for us, God's love is active. He not only declares his love for us; his attitudes and actions prove it. Describe what God has done — and is still doing — to express this everlasting love to his children.

- Exodus 15:13

- Psalm 94:18*

- Psalm 147:11*

- Hosea 14:4*

- Titus 3:4—7*

- 1 John 4:16—18

MORE ABOUT SIGNIFICANCE

Because of his great, active love for us, the Scriptures describe God as the Shepherd who "gathers the lambs in his arms and carries them close to his heart" (Isaiah 40:11). And King David asked, "When I consider your heavens, the work of your fingers, the moon and the stars, which you have set in place, what is man that you are mindful of him?... You made him a little lower than the heavenly beings and crowned him with glory and honor" (Psalm 8:3–5).

These verses point to humanity's importance to God, but what about our individual and personal significance to him? It's far easier to recognize our collective worth as human beings (we think the geniuses and famous names and humanitarians might upgrade our own doubtful status) than to stand alone and announce, "By myself, I am significant. I am irreplaceable to God."

But remarkably, this is the truth.

It is especially difficult for women to own this truth. We base our significance on doing and hope the activity will verify our value and lovability. We do not easily understand that just being a person created by God makes us deeply significant.

God made me in his image so that I dare to speak up about my uniqueness. — *Miriam Adeney*

5. Conduct an honest personal inventory. On what have you based your significance? Using a scale of 1 for "little significance," 2 for "moderate significance," and 3 for "high significance," indicate how much you've gauged your personal significance by the following:

- _____ Appearance
- _____ Awards and recognition
- _____ Children
- _____ Fitness
- _____ Friends
- _____ God
- _____ Health
- _____ Husband or boyfriend
- _____ Job
- _____ Money
- _____ Possessions
- _____ Social standing
- _____ Spiritual growth
- _____ Sports
- _____ Success
- _____ Volunteer activities
- _____ Other:

6. Thoughtfully and prayerfully review your "significance ratings" in #5. Then write an honest sentence that begins as follows: In my everyday life I primarily base my personal significance or identity on...

7. By comparison read the following verses and consider what God says about your significance. (Use the available spaces to jot notes about each verse.) Then write a few sentences that describe his opinion of your personal significance in the world.

- Deuteronomy 32:10—11*

- Psalm 71:6

- Psalm 139:13—16*

- Isaiah 44:2

- Isaiah 49:15—16*

- God says I am deeply significant because...

8. In the past, how have you responded to God's declaration of love for you?

9. How might you need to change your response to the Creator's love and actions toward you?

LOVING RESPONSES TO GOD

When we're willing to wrestle with our disbelief and eventually embrace a God-based significance, when we push beyond an intellectual understanding into the knowledge of the heart, it poignantly influences how we view ourselves and manage our lives. Instead of questioning our worth and berating our imperfections, we can consider ourselves magnificent works of art in progress, filled with meaning and the freedom to be who God created us to be.

Even more, we could accomplish nothing or everything admired by humanity (within biblical parameters) and keep peace within our souls. We hear the Creator's affirming whispers and know that our significance does not fluctuate with the circumstances. We stay God-centered and internally free. We find ourselves rooted in love and confidence instead of tossed by the wavering winds of accomplishment.

We also lovingly respond to God.

10. According to the following verses, how can we lovingly respond to God? In which ways do you already respond to him? Circle them. Which do you want to learn to express? Place a check next to them.

- Psalm 13:5–6*

- Psalm 143:8

- Micah 6:8*

- Luke 10:27

- John 14:21*

DESIRING TO PLEASE

When we rest in God's love and our significance to him, we naturally desire to please the one who so unconditionally accepts us. When we feel accepted for who we are, we are unafraid to be who he created us to be, or to do what he asks us to do. We become as children at play, risking everything and imagining anything because a loving parent protectively watches us from nearby.

11. What would you like to pursue if you felt secure in your significance to God (examples: a dream, a line of work, a relationship)?

12. What blocks you from pursuing this action?

13. What could "unblock" you from pursuing this action?

PUTTING FIRST THINGS FIRST

Understanding our unshakable significance before we attempt accomplishment anchors our souls in an order uncommon to this world. That is, we embrace our innate worth before we pursue our tasks and dreams. Then if circumstances point us in a direction we do not want, plan, or expect, our inner security doesn't crumble. We focus on God first, then everything else falls into perspective.

This means that whatever life serves us — times of productivity or seasons of fallowness, Olympian flexibility or confinement to a wheelchair, personal and professional highs or lows — we define ourselves by our significance to God rather than by what we do.

14. How has your life not turned out as you expected?

15. How could embracing your significance to God affect your unwanted circumstances?

TAKING THE BIG LEAP

If we at least faintly desire to embrace our innate worth, how do we start? It seems a long jump over the chasm between our gnawing uncertainties and such lavish self-esteem.

Although we'd prefer receiving step-by-step instructions from someone who already has mastered this principle, the learning process doesn't operate that way. It unfolds itself differently for each individual, and another simple reality confronts us at this point. As with everything else in life, we are not the ultimate controllers of this learning process. God is. We can pray, meditate on Scripture, listen to other people's stories, or attend seminars and Bible studies. But the most important action is *simply to ask God to reveal the truth to us in the manner he chooses.*

When we express a willingness to learn, God allows individual circumstances to teach us about our true worth, and when we release ourselves to his wisdom and trustworthiness, recognizing and cooperating with the process, the leap to significance grows less frightening. He often uses unexpected and even unwanted changes in circumstances — like an illness or a loss — to expose our misplaced beliefs and priorities.

It was for love that God created the world.
It was for love that God made man in his own image,
thus making him a partner in love, a being to whom
he speaks, who he loves like a son, and who can
answer him and love him like a father. — *Paul Tournier*

16. How might unwanted changes or circumstances be exposing your misplaced beliefs and priorities? Describe those beliefs and priorities.

17. Are you willing to learn and internalize the meaning of your true significance? If so, write out your request to God. Date and sign the prayer, offering it as a commitment to deeper spiritual growth.

Dear God,
I want to understand my significance to you because...

Signed:

Date:

18. What is the most important concept you've gleaned from this session?

OPTIONAL ACTIVITIES

1. This Bible study is based on the book, *Designing a Woman's Life*. Obtain the book and read chapter one entitled "Significance." Underline passages that speak personally to you.

2. Begin a private "response journal." After each session write out your candid responses to the text: your fears, hopes, relief, disbelief,

frustration, or any other feelings that surface. You don't have to share these pages with anyone, but they can chart your progress throughout the eight sessions.

You can also include lists, prayers, drawings, questions, Bible verses, or anything else that comes to mind. Don't edit yourself; write your thoughts with abandonment before a loving, accepting God.

3. Using a Bible concordance, locate and write out additional verses about God's love and loving responses to him.

4. If you struggle with understanding and accepting God's love, complete this sentence with as many examples as you can create. Repeat them to yourself each day, asking God to penetrate your soul with his love.

God's love is *not* like _____; it is like

_____.

(Example: God's love is *not* like a sledgehammer; it is like a comforting pillow.)

5. Write a letter to anyone who has damaged your sense of significance. Explain your feelings, but also forgive him or her. When you're finished writing, tear up the letter and discard it, marking a symbolic release from the negative opinions. As a reminder, record this event in your response journal.

6. This week watch for signs of your significance. Write down any comment or incident God might use to teach you about your true, biblically based significance.

7. Restate this verse in your own words, applying it to your life: "I praise you because I am fearfully and wonderfully made; your works are wonderful, I know that full well" (Psalm 139:14).

Next Session: Learn the meaning of purpose and how it can influence the world.

Purpose

Finding Our God-Intended Destiny

❧

[God] has given each of us the gift of life with a specific purpose in view.
To Him work is a sacrament, even what we consider
unimportant, mundane work.
For each of us, He does have a plan.
What joy to find it and even out of our helplessness,
let Him guide us in its fulfillment.

CATHERINE MARSHALL

A SIMPLE TRUTH

God created you to fulfill a unique purpose.

WORDS TO REMEMBER

"The LORD will fulfill his purpose for me." — Psalm 138:8

THE MEANING OF PURPOSE

I once spoke to a group of California women who meet monthly at seven in the morning to discuss integrating their faith and work. After reeling through a half-hour talk about "Letting God Direct Your Career," I wasn't sure if I'd made sense. While packing up my notes and handouts, though, a woman slid alongside me and said, "Thanks for the talk. I now realize what I've been doing wrong. I've been looking for a job instead of seeking a direction."

It intrigued me that she gleaned this idea from my speech because finding a life direction and purpose wasn't the topic. God's Spirit, ever surprising in his approach, must have whispered the truth to her, and I've no doubt that woman will discover her destiny. She already understands that when considering a life change, it helps to know her purpose before exploring an exact role or location.

We can learn from this woman's example because it's essential to define purpose before launching out after it. Simply defined, purpose is "the object for which something exists or is done; [the] end in view," and to do something "on purpose" is to tackle it "by design" or intentionally.[1]

So from a spiritual standpoint, pursuing our purpose means to discover our God-intended reason for being and to design our lives accordingly.

FIRST THOUGHTS

1. Describe a person you know (or know about) who seems certain of her purpose in life. What makes you think she knows her purpose? What are her attitudes and characteristics? What does she act like? How does she spend her time? What makes her different from other people?

2. Do you believe you have a unique purpose in life? Why, or why not?

3. What concerns you about searching for or clarifying your life's purpose? Before continuing this session, offer to God any fears or reservations you have. Write your prayer on the next page.

It would also help to discuss your concerns with a friend or study group members who will keep them confidential. Gather their insights and encouragement, along with their prayers.

Dear God,

These are my concerns about pursuing a life purpose...

Amen.

THREE INSTEAD OF ONE

In his booklet *How to Find Your Mission in Life*, Richard Bolles suggests we have not just one but three purposes or "reasons for being" and each one requires mastery before approaching the next. Briefly, these purposes are to live in the presence of God, to make this world a better place, and to exercise our greatest talent for God's work in the world.

Although this study focuses on the third purpose, Bolles's first two purposes merit exploration because they build a foundation for the outflow of our giftedness. Without this foundation, our intent to exercise a talent or purpose may collapse.[2]

OUR PURPOSES IN LIFE

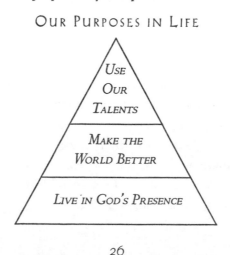

Use Our Talents

Make the World Better

Live in God's Presence

26

LIVING IN GOD'S PRESENCE

The Westminster catechism asks the question, "What is the chief and highest end of man?" and provides the still-relevant answer: "Man's chief and highest end is to glorify God, and fully to enjoy Him forever."[3] In basic terms this is what it means to fulfill the first purpose, to live in the presence of God. Our first priority revolves around knowing God; we spend time relating to him before we begin doing for him. Intimacy before action.

For those of us who have based our significance on accomplishing noteworthy tasks, this purpose statement sends something akin to shock through us. It sounds so passive, so devoid of the thrill of the hunt. But the Bible repeatedly advises us to intimately know the Purpose-Giver so we can express his purposes through us, so his purposes become our own.

4. According to these verses, how can we grow intimate with God?
   • Jeremiah 29:13

   • Matthew 6:33*

   • James 4:8*

5. Through the centuries devout Christians have described the ways they've "practiced the presence of God" or grown intimate with him. List some of those activities beneath their Scripture references.
   • Psalm 25:4*; Isaiah 30:21

   • 1 Samuel 15:22; James 1:22*

- Psalm 51:1–4, 7*

- 1 Samuel 3:10*; Psalm 95:6–8

- Psalm 119:99, 148*

- Psalm 119:11*, 52

- Matthew 7:7–11; 1 John 5:14–15*

- Jeremiah 15:17; Mark 1:35*

- Isaiah 12:5–6; Ephesians 5:19*

- Ephesians 5:20; 1 Thessalonians 5:18*

6. Review the spiritual disciplines in question #5. Circle one that you'd like to focus on for the duration of this course. How could you incorporate this discipline into your life?

7. During his time on earth Jesus practiced the presence of God, praying to and receiving instruction from his heavenly Father. Based on these verses, what were God's purposes for his son?

• Psalm 37:39–40*

• Luke 4:18–19

• Luke 19:10*

• John 10:10*

• John 10:28

• Galatians 4:4–5

8. How might pursuing your purpose contribute to fulfilling God's purposes in the world?

MAKING A BETTER WORLD

While the first purpose centers on our relationship with God, the second purpose — to make the world a better place — addresses our interaction with his creation and particularly humans, both the spiritually believing and unbelieving. But even cola commercials sing of making the world a better place, so how do we make a God-inspired difference?

When giving instructions to Moses, the Lord asked rhetorically, "What does the LORD your God ask of you?" Then he continued, "to fear [respect or reverence] the LORD your God, to walk in [obey] all his ways, to love him, to serve the LORD your God with all your heart and with all your soul, and to observe the LORD's commands" (Deuteronomy 10:12–13).

To respect, to obey, to love, to serve — these actions when practiced with a heart bowed to the Spirit's guidance, develop holy character within us and draw people to new life in God. But again, these actions flow toward God first, then spill out to others.

> *Having a purpose frees me from focusing on results.*
> *Instead, I am able to rest in the accomplishment*
> *of an underlying purpose that is not*
> *dependent on circumstances. — Cynthia Heald*

9. How can you first flow each of these actions — respecting, obeying, loving, serving — toward God? How can you direct these actions toward people, both the spiritually attuned and spiritually resistant? Write your ideas in the following places.

GOD   PEOPLE

- Respect

- Obey

- Love

- Serve

10. What other instructions does the Bible give for relating to the people in God's world? Aside from looking up these verses, you may want to add others to the list.

- Mark 16:15*

- Luke 6:37–38

- Ephesians 4:32*

- 1 Timothy 5:8

- Hebrews 10:25*

- Others:

BELONGING, UNIQUENESS, AND PURPOSE

Once we've embraced our first and second purposes, we can step up to the third purpose of exercising our greatest talent for God's work in the world.

However, when considering our individual purpose, a tension can stir within us. We want to identify with and belong to others, but at the same time we also long for personal distinctiveness. We are like other wives, clerks, athletes, mothers, artists, teachers, and executives, but how do we as individuals fill a role and express our giftedness in a way that nobody else does? What would the world miss if we didn't exist? And is it really possible to be one of a kind?

These often-silent questions expose an inner, though universal, craving to name our uniqueness, and God answers our questions with enduring love and patience.

11. Read 1 Corinthians 6:20* and Galatians 3:26–29*. How does God answer our need to belong?

12. As indicated by Psalm 139:13–16*; Matthew 10:30; John 10:3–6*; and Romans 12:6*, how has God fulfilled our need for uniqueness?

13. In God's family, how can we both belong and yet express our uniqueness? Answer this question by exploring the following scriptures. Can you think of other examples of our belonging and uniqueness? If so, add them to the list.

OUR BELONGING	OUR UNIQUENESS
• Romans 3:22—24*	• Romans 2:6—8*
• Psalm 48:14	• Job 23:10—12

• 1 Corinthians 12:12—27* (addresses both our belonging and uniqueness)

SECURING THE HEART

I can't think of any combination that secures a heart more than this: As Christians we are bound eternally to God the parent, who loves us unconditionally, and to spiritual brothers and sisters. At the same time we are free — even expected — to exercise our individuality and gift-edness.

14. In what ways do you want to belong? In what ways do you desire to be unique? Be specific, listing them below. Why are these facets of belonging and uniqueness important to you?

I Want to Belong   I Want to Be Unique

15. What personal giftedness do you want to express in your unique way?

ONE MORE THING

In the next session we'll explore how to develop the third purpose, but first consider one more idea. Often when women explore their giftedness, they ask, "Is it okay for a purpose to be something I love?" The answer is yes.

In fact, that is God's intent. He places talents and interests and spiritual gifts within us, then wraps up our purpose in them. And once we catch a glimpse of ourselves living fully and purposefully, there is no going back. Love and passion propel us forward.

16. Why would a woman think that God's purpose would *not* be something she loves?

17. Do you need to rectify this thinking for yourself? If so, how can you change your attitude?

18. What is the most intriguing fact you've learned in this session?

OPTIONAL ACTIVITIES

1. Read chapter two in *Designing a Woman's Life*, which explains more about our three purposes.

2. Create a "God Box" using a small box, a jar, an envelope, or other container. Write your specific fears about finding your purpose on pieces of paper and place them in the box. With this action you are giving these fears to God and letting him work out problem situations. You can use the God Box throughout this course, and even in the days beyond.

3. This week take time off with God. Practice one of the spiritual disciplines that creates intimacy with him. Record your thoughts and feelings from your time together.

4. Do you have a sense of belonging in your life? If not, discuss this with a trusted friend, mapping out ideas for helping you to belong.

5. Interview friends and family, asking, "What makes me unique?" Ask them to elaborate. Once you've compiled their responses, evaluate. Which comments sound accurate? Which were a surprise? What have you learned about yourself? Which comments could point to a life purpose?

6. Memorize the Bible verse in the opening "Words to Remember" section of this session.

7. Obtain one of the books in the "Exploration" section (bibliography) at the back of the book and read it. Compare its message with what you've learned from the Bible.

Next Session: Consider your uniqueness, and write a life purpose statement.

Authenticity

Staying True to the Woman Within

❧

What is in my hand?
Have I something to give?
Can I see a place where it is needed now?
These questions will help me
to know what I ought to do.

ELISABETH ELLIOT

A SIMPLE TRUTH

Purpose begins with understanding who God created you to be.

WORDS TO REMEMBER

"For God's gifts and his call are irrevocable." — Romans 11:29

BELIEVING IN OUR UNIQUENESS

Recently Diana and I treated ourselves to a comfort-food lunch because an organization offered another candidate the job she wanted. It stunned us because Diana is well qualified, and interviewers had implied she was a sure shot.

After some commiserating about job searches and rejection, I said, "Diana, it seems to me that before finding a job, you need to know your purpose. Do you know your life purpose?"

"No," she replied, looking sad. "Do you know yours?"

After several years of friendship it hadn't occurred to me to tell her. Sheepishly I said, "Yes. It's to publish the glad tidings."

I paused and then continued, "There are many ways I can publish the glad tidings. As a magazine editor, a book author, even a speaker (the broadest definition of "publish" being "to proclaim or make known"). But this purpose does require that I use my communication skills to encourage people with God's good news. Out of that purpose flow specific jobs, projects, audiences, or locations. So while my purpose remains constant, these other factors give it my unique spin and can change under God's guidance."

We then talked about what makes Diana unique, what delights her, and how these could hint at her life's purpose. Diana's eyes lit up. Just the thought of pursuing something she intrinsically loved pumped hope into her.

FIRST THOUGHTS

1. What makes you unique? List three personal characteristics.

2. What do you delight in doing, even if you're not accomplished at it?

3. Was it difficult for you to answer #1 or #2? Did any answers spark hope within you? Why, or why not?

TRUSTING THE WOMAN WITHIN

When we dare to claim our uniqueness and consider what delights us (without feeling unworthy or guilty about it), we step closer to becoming our authentic selves rather than who others tell us to be.

In college a friend dumbfounded me one day when she voiced her postgraduate goal to become a wife and mother. At the time it seemed an unremarkable objective for Jan, a bright and gifted person. After all, we approached adulthood in the early 1970s when our culture awakened to diversified career choices for women. Couldn't Jan become a businesswoman, an environmentalist, or a teacher?

Absolutely not. Jan followed her heart and after graduation married a man intent on youth ministry, and she settled into a modest, domestic lifestyle. Through the years her inner certainty deepened in proportion to her growing family — despite motherhood's everyday frustrations and the devastating loss of a newborn son. Observing her life, I realized I'd been misguided to think that homemaking was less a career or calling than any other profession. I also admired that Jan had listened to her soul.

> *The calling of God is a distinctive calling.*
> *The commissioning is always personal; it never stops at*
> *being general. Its objective is always precise; never merely*
> *haphazard or undefined. — Watchman Nee*

When we set out to discover a life purpose, we embark on a journey within, for to understand our reason for being is to recognize the shape of our souls. For Christians, the soul shapes in the hands of God, who indwells the spiritually surrendered believer with his Spirit.

When we stay in tune with this Spirit, listening to the woman within can synchronize with hearing from the Creator. But for the Holy Spirit to reveal God's truth in concert with the human soul, we must spiritually plumb our inner person and be convinced that God can and does speak to hearts.

4. The soul often has been defined as a combination of the mind, will, and emotions — the nonphysical part of a person that thinks, wills, and feels. The psalmists frequently mentioned the soul in their writings. According to these verses, what part does the soul play in a relationship with God?

• Psalm 19:7*

• Psalm 25:1

- Psalm 35:9*

- Psalm 42:2

- Psalm 63:8*

- Psalm 104:35*

5. Based on these verses, how does the devil attack the soul? How can we thwart the devil's attempts?

SATAN'S ATTACKS	OUR RESPONSE
▪ 1 Peter 5:8	▪ 1 Peter 5:9
▪ Ephesians 6:11–12*	▪ Ephesians 6:13–18*

SOUL AND SPIRIT IN HARMONY

The nineteenth-century Quaker teacher Hannah Whitall Smith described four timeless ways to discern God's voice speaking to our souls. In *The Christian's Secret to a Happy Life*, she explained that God speaks through the Scriptures, providential circumstances, the convictions of our higher judgment, and the inward impressions of the Holy Spirit on our minds. Hannah taught Christians to distinguish God's voice by testing these four influences for harmony.

She said, "His voice will always be in harmony with itself, no matter in how many different ways He may speak. The voices may be many, the message can be but one."[1] This test for harmony can help us learn to trust the woman within.

6. How can you test these "voices" when working to discern your life purpose?
   - The Scriptures

   - Providential circumstances

   - Convictions of your higher judgment

   - Inward impressions of the Holy Spirit

BREAKING DOWN BARRIERS

When we search for harmony in God's direction, it also sharpens our awareness of the blocks to God's voice expressed to the woman within. Not only can these blocks hinder us from discovering our purpose, but they also can diffuse the effectiveness of that purpose when we're in the thick of fulfilling it.

7. Read Psalm 95:7–8*. What can create a block to hearing God's voice and listening to the woman within?

8. What specifically could keep you from hearing God's voice?

9. According to 1 John 1:9*, how can we overcome a block to hearing God's voice within? Do you need to apply this principle to anything listed in #8? If so, what?

AUTHENTICATING OUR UNIQUENESS

When with the Holy Spirit's influence we listen to and trust the woman within, when we're so hungry for authenticity that we confront what needs internal attention and correction, we open a channel for hearing and confirming our purpose. At the same time, pinpointing a purpose is not so ethereal that only the mystical and monastic can do it. Much of our purpose already resides within us; again, we only need to look honestly within and ask questions.

The key is truthfulness. We need to be true *to* ourselves by being truthful *about* ourselves. No holding back. No answers that reflect who we think we *should be* rather than who we *really are*. No worrying about what others will think.

> *We can be confident in our uniqueness.*
> *To become the one I am created to be,*
> *isn't that my great work in life? — Ingrid Trobisch*

Once we choose to be truthful and authentic, the questions are so basic they could surprise us because we probably already know bits of the answers. *What are my talents? What are my dreams? What is my calling?* Answered individually, these questions provide insight; melded together and confirmed by God, they ignite purpose, pleasure, and passion.

Yes, pleasure and passion. Contrary to hedonistic or puritanical viewpoints, these are the holy results of living authentically, of staying true to the woman within and flowing in God's uniquely designed purpose. Christ promises us an *abundant* life (John 10:10), and when we pursue the truth about ourselves, it sets us free to enjoy living. But it is not for our pleasure only. In the movie *Chariots of Fire*, the track star Eric Liddell confided that when he ran, he felt God's pleasure.[2]

10. Read Philippians 2:12–13*. How do we approach finding and fulfilling our purpose? Why?

USING OR LOSING TALENTS

What are my talents? When a woman protests and says, "But I have no talent," I can almost hear the cosmic *Whack!* of her slapping God's face. How it must grieve him to hear this. After lovingly creating each of us as unique individuals, after molding us in his image of giftedness, we reject his spectacular handiwork.

Everyone possesses talent. Some people received more talent than we did; some talents garner more public recognition than others. To jealously compare ourselves with others and mourn our "lesser" or "nonexistent" talent shoves away the satisfaction of fulfilling our own purpose. Besides, the "who gets what" decisions belong to God; our responsibility is to exercise the talents he gave us.

11. Christ emphasized this stewardship in the parable of the talents. Although the parable speaks of money, it serves as a metaphor for the use of our God-endowed abilities. Read this story in Matthew 25.14 29*. Summarize Christ's teaching about using or losing our talents.

ASSESSING OUR TALENTS

If we still have trouble thinking of ourselves as talented, we can ask, "What am I good at doing?" These are the things physical (working with numbers or coordinating colors and fabrics) or relational (encouraging people in their marriages or helping them heal wounds) that we do well and the work satisfies us. They include things we do now and perhaps things we stopped doing somewhere along the path to today.

Richard Bolles claims that God has already revealed our mission to us by "writing it in our members" or our personal makeup. He adds, "We are to begin deciphering our unique Mission by studying our talents and skills, and more particularly which ones (or One) we most rejoice to use."[3]

12. What are your talents? List those you currently use and ones you're not exercising now.

Exercising Spiritual Gifts

In addition to our innate talents, God endows spiritual gifts when he fills us with the Holy Spirit. These gifts, which are manifestations of the Spirit and supernatural in nature, may enhance our innate talents with a spiritual anointing or add to our repertoire of abilities. Many Christians receive a cluster of spiritual gifts rather than just one, but the Holy Spirit determines these allotments, not us.

Whatever spiritual gifts we receive, God wants us to use them to help his children. And when we assess both our talents and spiritual gifting, we're only a step away from defining our purpose.

13. Read 1 Corinthians 12*, then list the gifts the Holy Spirit gives to God's children.

14. Based on the above scriptures and your understanding of the Holy Spirit's gifts, list your spiritual gifts.

DANCING OUR DREAMS

What are my dreams? Disregarding real or imaginary constraints, how would we like to use our talents? What desires are tucked in the heart? What would we love to spend a lifetime doing? What would bring joy and meaning and contentment?

What accomplishment stays buried for fear we're incapable of achieving it or that somebody might laugh at the idea? Risk pulling it out and mulling it over. God gives us the desires of our hearts. Could it be we've repressed a dream that is actually his purpose for us?

God-inspired dreams blend both the realistic and the impossible. They are obtainable enough that we can imagine ourselves, with our innate though inexperienced talents, pursuing them. They are impossible enough that we need God's power and intervention to reach them.

15. What are your unfulfilled dreams? Describe them below, no matter how impossible they seem to you.

CONSIDERING OUR CALLING

What is my calling? To answer this question, we consider not only what we do but whom we're to serve with our talents and dreams. My favorite explanation of calling originated with novelist Frederick Buechner: "The place God calls you to is the place where your deep gladness and the world's deep hunger meet."[4] God doesn't gift us with talent just to lavish it on ourselves. He expects us to use that talent for his service, and his kingdom focuses on redeeming people.

Frequently a calling falls in step with the natural course of our lives; other times it radically uproots us from familiar surroundings. A calling can last a lifetime; it can last for only a specified period. The direction and duration depend on God's desire for each individual, so it's vital to ask him periodically to reaffirm our calling and amend it with his delightful detours. However, a calling, though it stretches our talents and challenges our priorities, does not fall outside of our desires and giftedness. Calling dwells within our overall purpose.

16. To whom do you feel called or compelled to serve with your talents? Why?

DEFINING THE PASSION

Author and consultant Marsha Sinetar suggests that to find an enduring life purpose, we can ask ourselves, "What's worth doing?" "What attracts me?" "What makes me willing to stretch and struggle?"[5] I would add to these, "What stirs my passion?" When we've answered these questions and striven to stay true to the woman within, we can prayerfully define our purpose by composing a purpose statement.

Many ways exist to structure a purpose statement, but it's effective to describe the purpose in terms general enough to span a lifetime but specific enough to guide goal and decision making. It should also state the people we want to reach and the desired outcome of serving them.

These are examples of stated purposes:

• To compose music that draws people to the beauty in God's soul.

• To help people eat healthily, freeing them to live as God's temples.

• To assist the Spirit in healing children's wounded hearts so they can grow into whole and spiritually alive adults.

• To manage finances so families and companies align with biblical principles regarding money.

• To intercede in prayer for downtrodden people around the globe so their physical and spiritual needs are met.

If at this juncture we're still uncertain about our inner selves, it is better to at least experiment with a stated purpose than to continue an ineffectual, meandering lifestyle. God honors faith, and we can ask him to "establish the work of our hands" (Psalm 90:17) when it feels as though we're bumbling along.

17. Psalm 37:23–24* can assure you about your journey toward purpose. What does it promise?

18. Prayerfully review your talents (#12), spiritual gifts (#14), dreams (#15), and calling (#16). Which do you sense could contribute to your life purpose? Circle these.

Which might only be employed as hobbies or occasional activities? Underline them.

19. Based on the above information, write a purpose statement for yourself.

My purpose is to...

20. If you could only remember one idea from this session, what would it be?

OPTIONAL ACTIVITIES

1. Read chapter three entitled "Authenticity" in the *Designing a Woman's Life* book.

2. Conduct a soul-searching authenticity inventory, answering the following questions.

- Have I been living authentically? Why, or why not?
- Are there talents I've abandoned that I'd like to use again? If so, what are they?
- Is there a dream I'd like to pursue but am afraid to try? If so, why?
- What will I gain if I become more true to who God created me to be? What will I lose? How do I feel about this?

▪ What could be my first step toward greater authenticity?

3. Read the account of Moses and the burning bush in Exodus 3–4:17. Then answer these questions:

▪ What is the significance of God's question to Moses, "What is in your hand?"

▪ What were Moses' excuses for not following God's purpose?

▪ What were God's replies to Moses?

▪ What are your reasons for not following God's purpose?

▪ What might be God's reply to you? If possible, base your answers on Scripture.

4. Draw a picture of yourself as a child, doing the things you loved to do. How does this picture relate to who you are today? Does the drawing unveil anything you've left behind that might be part of your life's purpose? Describe this lost talent, attitude, or activity in your response journal. Write out ideas for recapturing this talent, attitude, or activity.

5. Take activity #4 a step farther and spend an hour doing a childhood activity you left behind. Does this activity tap into joy and passion? If so, it could indicate an aspect of your life purpose as an adult.

6. Imagine what it would be like to live a fully authentic life, pursuing your purpose. How do you act, look, and feel? What do you say and believe?

7. Read the description of yourself to a supportive friend. Ask her to add to it, filling in aspects you've overlooked or feel reluctant to imagine.

8. Enroll in a seminar or course related to your purpose, preparing yourself for the future.

Next Session: Begin cultivating a vision based on your purpose.

Vision

Seeing and Believing the Unseen

To believe in something not yet proved
and to underwrite it with our lives:
it is the only way we can keep the future open.

LILLIAN SMITH

A SIMPLE TRUTH

God births purpose-filled vision in the hearts of his children.

WORDS TO REMEMBER

"The [vision] awaits an appointed time.... Though it linger, wait for it."
— Habakkuk 2:3

A GOOD IMAGINATION

For moments I stand still in the meadow, wondering where its gentle breezes will nudge me next. I've come to the French countryside to wander, to adore the summertime and its glories — to shake off the din of too much living.

And during this pause, I hear music.

As faint as the wisps of wind, I strain for the flute's melody and follow it. Quickening my pace, I hear the notes grow stronger, more lyrical. Then cresting a small hill I spot two peasant-dressed, bare-footed girls huddled together in a valley below, the older one creating music beyond her years and the younger leaning in close and intently observing.

I stop suddenly but quietly, so they can't detect me. I long to join them, casting away responsibility and pretending nothing matters but this magical interlude. But then I turn my head, and much too soon I'm back to brushing my teeth.

I'm not really in France; I'm standing in my bathroom, looking at a print that hangs on the wall above an oak bureau. Actually, I've never even traveled to France, but encountering the golden-framed girls and their flute, I imagine myself there. I can see myself in a country inn or a Parisian bistro, and I know that someday I will visit the land of the Louvre and flirty waiters named Pierre.

Do my bathroom musings about France seem silly and far-fetched?

Welcome to the world of vision. In this realm, one woman's dream is another woman's foolishness. The satirist Jonathan Swift said, "Vision is the art of seeing things invisible,"[1] and some of history's greatest visionaries have been mistaken for lunatics instead of artists and saints. Yet we cannot live without vision. Vision — imagining what can be — keeps us physically and spiritually alive.

FIRST THOUGHTS

1. Do you consider yourself to be a visionary person? Why, or why not?

2. What do you daydream about? Could this fantasy be the seeds of a God-intended vision related to your purpose? Keep it in mind as you complete this session.

3. What would you like God to teach you about vision?

PURPOSEFUL, SPIRITUAL VISION

Once we determine our life purpose, we need spiritual vision to fulfill it. Spiritual vision believes in the possibilities for pursuing our purpose, motivating us to meet our greatest potential by accomplishing God's work in the world.

When we open ourselves to vision, we can think of it as narrowing down or further clarifying our life purpose. A vision tells us the specific work we're to accomplish and the particular group of people we're to reach. It comprises the practical, everyday things we do to accomplish our purpose.

At the same time, spiritual vision is "the stuff that dreams are made of."[2] With God anything is possible, and usually we don't dream expansively enough about how to fulfill our purpose.

4. What spiritual vision did these biblical people follow?
   • Samuel in 1 Samuel 3

   • Esther in Esther 2:15–18; 3:10–4:16*

   • Jeremiah in Jeremiah 1

5. Do you know people who have followed a God-given vision, big or small? Describe their experiences and what you can learn from it.

6. How do we know that, with God, we can envision and believe in the "impossible dream"?
   • Matthew 19:26

   • Matthew 21:21—22*

PERISHING WITHOUT VISION

The Bible says that without a vision, people perish (Proverbs 29:18, KJV). To keep our souls vibrant, we need something to hope for, believe in, and live for even if the vision tarries or isn't fulfilled in our lifetime.

Yet even sensing this soul-felt need, we can travel through life without vision. We can lack spiritual vision even though we know something within us is missing. Or we can fail to follow through on a vision that God offers us. Whatever the case, the pursuit of vision doesn't just happen to us. It is a choice.

Child of God, learn a family secret. God specializes in things we think are totally impossible. — *Charles Swindoll*

7. How did these people fail to pursue spiritual vision? What attitudes and actions did they have in common?
   • King Saul in 1 Samuel 15:16—23*

   • Jonah in Jonah 1:1—2*

   • Saul and Jonah exhibited these attitudes and actions:

8. According to the following Bible verses, what can keep us from "seeing" a spiritual vision and fulfilling it? Can you think of others to add to this list?

- Psalm 56:11

- Psalm 66:18*

- Proverbs 16:18*

- Others:

9. Do you erect barriers to cultivating spiritual vision? If so, what are they? From the following list, circle the ones that apply and then add any others.

- Besetting sin
- Busyness
- Competitiveness
- Disbelief
- Emotional wounds
- Fear of failure
- Fear of success
- Health limitations
- Jealousy
- Lack of discipline
- Lack of finances
- Laziness
- Low self-esteem
- People's opinions
- Resentment
- Self-pity
- Social standing
- Pride
- Worry
- Wrong location
- Other:

10. What are your feelings about these barriers? Be specific.

FEELING AND FACING FEARS

Probably we all can find our excuses on this list, plus add a few unusual barriers of our own. But what creates the resistance?

Mostly it's fear. We can fear what vision will cost us in time, money, energy, sacrifice, preparation, and reputation. If we step into a vision, we could feel unprepared for the challenge and defenseless against the unknown. We prefer familiarity over risk.

However, clinging to this preference misses God's best for us. He designed us to be purposeful, granting us the capacity to grow socially, emotionally, spiritually, and intellectually throughout our lives. Jesus never taught us to be comfortable and maintain the status quo. He commanded us to go, grow, and change the world.

> *We have to be braver than we think we can be,*
> *because God is constantly calling us to be more*
> *than we are.* — *Madeleine L'Engle*

Blessedly, God wants to break down our fear-filled defenses — whatever might block our vision — so we can receive his love and offer it to others. His end goal is the redemption of people, and with this objective in mind, we can revel in our resulting defenselessness. It is the open, willing heart that God fills with vision and uses in his service.

11. Review the items you circled in #9. Are any of these barriers based on fear? If so, what scares you?

12. Read Luke 22:31—32* and Romans 8:13—15*. Where does fear originate?

13. What spiritual resources are available for us to overcome fear?
  • Joshua 1:6—9*

  • Psalm 56:3*

  • John 14:27*

  • James 4:7*

  • 1 Peter 3:13—16

  • 1 John 4:18

14. How could you overcome these barriers (#8 and #9) to spiritual vision, especially those motivated by fear?

FILLING UP WITH VISION

I'm not suggesting that when we embrace a vision, we never feel afraid. I'm recommending that instead of saying "I can't," we declare, "I can't by myself, but with God's help I can."

This statement offers our fear to God and confesses our willingness to move forward by faith, despite our misgivings. Because he granted us the freedom to choose, God needs our willingness to start the process, but that is all. He takes over from there. Though fearful, we can comfort ourselves with the fact that God fulfills his promises; he makes good on the visions he plants in his children's anxious hearts.

15. When in repentance we accept his grace and forgiveness, God fills our spirit with his, but that is only the beginning. Paul wrote in Ephesians 3:16—21* about the overflowing abundance available to the followers of God through Jesus Christ. In each of these verses (16—20), what does God offer to his children?

- Verse 16

- Verse 17

- Verse 18

- Verse 19

- Verse 20

UNIMAGINED VISITATIONS

Not only does God give us his Spirit, he affords us inner power and strength. Not only does he lavish us with immeasurable love, he fills us with everything available in himself and from his resources. Not only does he answer our requests, he exceeds our expectations. This is the essence of spiritual vision: *God filling us with himself and then playing a game of one-upmanship on our dreams.* He longs to fulfill our purpose in breathtaking ways we don't even imagine.

He also can reveal a spiritual vision to us in unusual ways. True to his creative nature, God uses methods that fit the individuals and circumstances involved, from the dramatic confrontation to a quiet knowing within.

16. In Scripture we read stories in which the Lord employed dramatic means to impart vision. How did God reveal his vision to these people?
   • Elijah in 1 Kings 19:11–13*

   • Isaiah in Isaiah 6:1–8

   • Saul in Acts 9:3–9*

17. These announcements were exotic measures for unusual tasks, but God still uses unusual ways to get our attention. Are you open to God using supernatural power to reveal his vision for you? Why, or why not?

18. God's way of leading one person cannot be the measuring stick for how others hear from him. Again, God speaks to individuals in

individual ways. There are people who have prayed, searched the Bible, listed the possibilities, and accomplished what most appealed to them — and have faithfully carried out a vision. When sparking vision, God specializes in diversity. From these verses, what other ways can people discern God's vision for them?

- Proverbs 12:15*

- Mark 11:24*

- John 7:17

- 2 Timothy 3:16*

19. Frequently a vision births from our particular life experiences. Do you have a life experience that could ignite a spiritual vision within you? A vision that would serve others? If so, briefly explain it below.

BY SEARCHING AND LISTENING

By searching for and listening to God, we can find the vision we're to follow. However, as we mold a vision, we're not to use a secular mind-set that insists showmanship, big productions, and high visibility are what's best. We're to listen for what God has prepared for us, within the abilities, personality, and circumstances that constitute our purpose.

In his upside-down kingdom, the small and humble outreaches can deserve the most praise. What matters is that we find our vision and follow it wholeheartedly. With God, it is not prestige that counts but the condition of a heart.

20. How might you be tempted toward a secular mind-set in determining your vision? How can you stay aware and avoid this?

WHAT THE LORD REQUIRES

The Father-Creator wants to fill us with vision, and if we understand and trust his good ways, this vision will captivate and motivate us through the seasons of its development. A God-endowed vision is a not-yet-realized goal we feel *honored* to pursue, for it wraps together our talents, dreams, calling, personality — our very soul — and ignites our purpose. But be warned: As with accepting God's salvation, a vision requires *giving all of ourselves,* and perhaps this is why people don't follow their dreams. We're in the habit of hiding and holding back parts of ourselves. Embarking on God's adventure requires that we grow, change, and improve along with it, discarding what hinders effectiveness and accepting new ways of being.

21. What does God require of us as we pursue a spiritual vision?
   ▪ Psalm 25:15*

- 1 Thessalonians 5:16—22*

- Hebrews 10:24—25

- Hebrews 10:35

- Hebrews 11:6*

EMBRACING OUR VISION

As we embrace a vision, we also keep in mind that its duration can vary. We may pursue one vision for a lifetime, or over a lifetime God may ask us to pursue several.

For example, our purpose may be to present the gospel to children, and within that framework, we follow a vision to develop Sunday school classes for urban, grade-school children. At another time, God may call us to volunteer at a year-round camp for single-parent kids, and we work with the junior high group. Same purpose, different vision.

22. As best you can tell, what is God's vision for your life now? Be as specific as possible.

23. What is the most significant spiritual principle that you've learned in this session?

OPTIONAL ACTIVITIES

1. Read the chapter entitled "Vision" in the *Designing a Woman's Life* book.

2. Write out a detailed description of you pursuing your vision. Also draw a picture of you living this vision. Share this description and picture with a confidante, then tuck them away for future reference. Later it will be interesting to compare your description with reality.

3. Read a biography of a woman who pursued a personal vision. What can you learn from her life, both positive and negative?

4. Interview a woman who has pursued and obtained her vision. Ask questions that will help you effectively pursue your dream. Could this woman mentor you through your visionary pursuits? Be courageous. Ask her.

5. Create a simple, five-year plan for making your vision a reality. Include physical and spiritual goals, plus how you can accomplish them.

6. Start a "visionary support group" of women who are pursuing their dreams. Meet once a month to pray together, discuss progress, strategize jumping over hurdles, and generally encourage one another.

7. Collect quotes from people who have pursued their vision. Write them on index cards or Post-It Notes and place them in strategic places around your home or office. Memorize the ones that motivate you.

Next Session: Work on focusing your life to accomplish your purpose.

Focus

Pursuing What Matters the Most

How we spend our days is, of course,
how we spend our lives.
There is no shortage of good days.
It is good lives that are hard to come by.

A N N I E   D I L L A R D

A SIMPLE TRUTH

A fulfilled purpose stems from a focused, obedient life.

WORDS TO REMEMBER

"Let us fix our eyes on Jesus, the author and perfecter of our faith." —
Hebrews 12:2

A STORY OF TWO WOMEN

Clare Boothe Luce grabbed for everything she could squeeze out of life
and its accomplishments. Born in the tenements, at an early age Clare
vowed to abandon obscurity and become memorable through her work
and associations.

That she did. In the 1930s she rose to managing editor of *Vanity
Fair*. Through her later marriage to Henry Luce, she influenced the
man who created the TIME, INC., publishing empire. Together they
grew powerfully rich.

But for Clare that wasn't enough. After stints in magazine publishing she also wrote much-acclaimed plays, served two terms in
Congress, and became the United States ambassador to Italy.

To the public, there was nothing Clare couldn't do, nothing she
didn't own. In private, her friends and family observed that she relent-
lessly pursued what she never achieved: inner peace and satisfaction.
"One achieves so much less than one's expectations," she said toward
the end of her life. "I was thinking at one time of writing my memoirs
and calling it *Confessions of an Unsuccessful Woman*. I've done too
many things and it doesn't stack up."[1]

Compare Clare's story to Evelyn Harris Brand's life.

Evelyn enjoyed ribbon-and-lace comfort as the daughter of a
prosperous, turn-of-the-century London merchant. Then at thirty

she heard about the great physical and spiritual needs in India and committed herself to serve there. In that country she married Jesse Brand, a handsome visionary who shared her passion for the poor mountain people. The couple set up housekeeping in "the mountains of death" and pursued their vision.

Evelyn's dream of marital togetherness didn't last for a lifetime, though. At age forty-four Jesse died from blackwater fever. When the mission board expected Evelyn then to leave the hills, she refused. Her antidote for grief was continuing the work Jesse loved.

At retirement age she quit the mission board and moved to another mountain, supported by a family inheritance. "It's terribly marvelous to be used by God," she wrote. "Granny Brand" served in the hills another thirty years before she died there at age ninety-five.[2]

While Clare lived glamorously and broadly, she died bitter and alone. Evelyn, though poor and not widely traveled, finished her life satisfied and triumphant. Aside from their obvious spiritual differences, Evelyn mastered an element of success Clare never did: the ability to focus. Clare jumped restlessly from interest to interest; Evelyn pursued one constant goal.

Their contrasting conclusions present a lesson: Purpose without focus stacks up to no purpose at all.

> In the long run men hit only what they aim for.
> — Henry David Thoreau

Focus is "to fix or settle on one thing; [to] concentrate"[3] on it to the exclusion of other interests, no matter how worthy, intriguing, and rewarding those pursuits might be. Focus requires that we funnel our energy into fulfilling one overarching purpose, one compelling vision — if not for a lifetime, at least one at a time.

FIRST THOUGHTS

1. Does the word *focus* connote a positive or negative meaning to you? Why?

2. In regard to your life purpose, how focused are you? On a scale of 1 to 10, with 1 as "very *unfocused*" and 10 as "very focused," what number would you assign yourself?

3. Why are you currently this focused or unfocused?

THE LOGICAL NEXT STEP

Focus enables our God-given dreams to come true and is among the most arduous and rewarding life choices we'll ever face. However, if we've discovered our true purpose — a purpose that wells from the soul and spills over with passion — focus becomes the logical next step.

As we fall more in love with our purpose, we willingly ferret out the distractions, the unnecessary elements that diffuse our energy, attention, and ability to reach a purposeful goal, letting much of the world pass by at a distance. We grow attuned to the Holy Spirit within, hearing a melody composed just for us and hushing the cacophony without.

4. The following verses are statements from people who focused on their purpose. Summarize their words in the provided spaces.

• Jesus in Luke 22:42 and John 6:38*

• The apostles in Acts 5:27–29*

• Paul in Philippians 3:13–14*

• Peter in 1 Peter 1:13–14

• John in 1 John 2:15–17

5. What attitudes did these focused people share?

6. Do you know anyone who expresses these same attitudes? Describe what makes that person focused. Is there anything about her or him you would like to emulate? Explain.

PRUNING BACK OUR LIVES

Although focused people express passion and certainty, their single-mindedness doesn't emerge without struggle. In fact, focus usually births itself by pruning our lives. And if we possess various interests and abilities (as most of us do), we repeatedly weather the frustration of choosing the best over the good.

7. Jesus taught about pruning the branches of a vine. According to John 15:1—2*, what is the purpose of pruning our lives?

8. John 15:3—8* continues the teaching about pruning. What other points about fruitfulness did Jesus stress?

9. Why would personal pruning — be it character or schedules — sometimes feel uncomfortable or painful?

10. List below your major involvements: personal, professional, religious, community, etc. Circle the activities that already contribute to your purpose.
- Personal

- Professional

- Religious

- Community

- Other

11. To effectively pursue your purpose, list activities that need to be added to your schedule.

12. Review the list in #10. To better focus on your purpose, what activities will you need to cut? Place an "x" by them.

PASSION VERSUS ADDICTION

When we begin to focus on our purpose and vision, it's necessary to incorporate balance, distinguishing between healthy sacrifice and debilitating obsession. "Many competent women have a difficult time distinguishing between passion and workaholism," cautions psychologist Anne Wilson Schaef. "Many of our role models for success are people who were willing to be devoured by their work. This is confusing to us. True passion and doing what is important for us to do does not require us to destroy ourselves in the process. In fact, it is when passion gets distorted to compulsivity that it is destructive."

She suggests this credo for compulsion-prone women: "My passion feeds me. My addictiveness devours me. There is a great difference
between the two."4 Accordingly, if we use our life purpose to alter
negative moods, prove our self-worth, or avoid what's painful, we've
crossed the line from passion into addiction. We're seeking serenity
from an object, event, or accomplishment instead of God.

13. The lists below note some differences between passion and addiction. As it relates to you, list other differences between the two. Ask
yourself, "How would I behave if I pursued something with passion?
How would I behave if I turned it into an addiction?" For reference,
you may want to consider food, work, love, money, and other things
or relationships we tend to abuse.

Passion	Addiction
• Feeds the soul	• Starves the soul
• Brings a fuller, happier person to relationships	• Leads to discontentment and isolation
• Serves God with an open, imaginative heart	• Shuts down vision and spirituality
• Creates and keeps boundaries	• Doesn't create boundaries
• Leads to healthy self-esteem	• Leads to poor self-esteem
• Takes time off; balances work with leisure	• Requires constant stimulation; forgets balance and leisure
• Other examples:	• Other examples:

14. Review the lists in #13. Circle what describes you. Have you circled
anything that needs attention so it doesn't turn into an addiction? If
so, what can you do about it?

THE RELATIONSHIP PRIORITY

People who stay balanced understand the priority of relationships, even though they're focused on a passionate life purpose. The book *The Addictive Personality* outlines four natural relationships we turn to for support, nurture, guidance, love, and emotional and spiritual growth. These relationships include family and friends, a spiritual Higher Power (whom we know to be God), self, and community. If we don't develop healthy relationships in these areas, we turn to other sources to meet our needs, and seeds of addiction root within us.[5]

15. On a scale of 1 for "no relationship" to 10 for "healthy relationship," how do you rate yourself on these relationships?
   - _____ Community   - _____ God
   - _____ Family   - _____ Self
   - _____ Friends

16. To balance your life, are there relationships that need alteration? If so, which one(s) and why?

COMMITMENT THROUGH OBEDIENCE

From a biblical standpoint, focus translates to obeying what God asks us to do. "God continually challenges us to act on our commitment. What will we do with God's instruction? How will we build into our lives the active demonstration of commitment through obedience? How will we handle what God has shown us?" asks Martha Thatcher, a spiritual mentor to women.[6]

Hopefully, we will obey his prompting to focus on what matters the most, to keep our eyes off diversions and on purposeful vision.

17. In the Bible God clarified for his children the rewards of obedience to him. What were those rewards?
- Deuteronomy 30:2—3*

- Job 36:11*

- Isaiah 1:19

- Jeremiah 7:23*

18. Even though these promises were delivered to people in the Bible, do you think any of them apply to you and your purpose? Explain.

Obedience through Risk

However God directs us, he eventually asks us to risk as we pursue our vision. What looks like risk to one person may not appear as risk to others, so we can experience a sense of aloneness in our initial, shaky steps toward focus. This is God arranging circumstances so we trust him, and only him, during a winnowing process.

19. If we're going to follow through on risk, how are we to live? Read 2 Corinthians 5:7*.

20. When you follow your purpose and vision, what risk(s) will you need to take? How do you feel about this?

21. Focus is risky business when people don't understand our decisions. How can you prepare family, friends, colleagues, or others for the changes that focus and risk will bring? What do you need to consider about their feelings and everyday lives?

FREEDOM AND CHANGE

We can test our focus by asking, "Am I making steady progress in fulfilling my life purpose and current vision?" If we answer no, then the follow-up question becomes "What needs to change?"

When we enter the change process, we can emphasize what we'll lose to the exclusion of what we'll gain. If this mind-set fits us, we first need to adjust our attitude about change. When we implement change in favor of focus, we set ourselves free to reach God's best and highest purpose for us, meshed with the fulfillment of our desires. What could be more rewarding than that? Why would we resist change when it ushers in our dreams?

We resist change when we're focused on worldly security, clutching what we can see instead of visualizing who we can be. But this is a false security, based on the temporal and unpredictable. We can cling to jobs, homes, titles, habits, schedules, locations, relationships, involvements, and an abundance of *things* as if they constitute what's truly rewarding and eternal.

Consequently, we must see through spiritual eyes to detect what has become a proverbial albatross, weighing us down and drowning purposeful progress. With spiritual eyesight, we identify as sin whatever hinders God's design.

22. When you begin to focus, what will you lose? What will you gain? How do you feel about this?

- I will lose...

- I will gain...

- I feel...

23. To dissolve our resistance to change, our clinging to the physical or sinful, what does the Bible advise us to do in Hebrews 12:1—2*?

24. As Jesus did, we set aside purpose-hindering weights to focus on the joy set before us — the joy of being all God created us to be, the wonder of doing all he's called us to do. What purpose-hindering weights do you need to set aside? How can you do this?

25. According to Philippians 4:13, why is this change possible?

26. What Bible verse from this session is the most meaningful to you?

OPTIONAL ACTIVITIES

1. Read chapter five entitled "Focus" in the book *Designing a Woman's Life.*

2. In the *Designing* book, review the section titled "The Rhythm of Responsibilities" (page 92) and answer these questions:
   • What are my main responsibilities and priorities in life?
   • How do I relate these to my purpose?
   • What schedule would suit me best as I pursue my purpose?

3. Read the "Accepting the Interruptions" section (page 96) in the *Designing* book. Then consider these questions:

- What are the usual interruptions to my schedule?
- Which of these can be eliminated? Which cannot?
- How can I develop a healthy attitude toward these interruptions?
- How can I creatively include these interruptions in my daily routines?

4. Enroll in a time-management course, or read a book about ordering your life.

5. In the *Designing* book, read the section titled "A Time for Everything" (page 97), or read King Solomon's poetry in Ecclesiastes 3:1—8.

- In this season of your life, what is there time for?
- What is there not time for?
- What can you anticipate adding to your days in the future?

6. Write your own poem patterned after Solomon's words in Ecclesiastes 3:1—8. Begin with "There is a time for everything. A time for..." and write a few lines that apply to your life.

7. Create a poster that states your life purpose and the primary involvements it entails. Hang the poster in your office or kitchen to remind you and others of your focus and priorities.

8. Gather family or friends and tell them about your focus. Listen to their feedback about how to arrange your life, both in light of your purpose and relationship with them.

Next Session: Find out how brokenness can enhance your quest for purpose.

Brokenness

Facing Pain and Weakness

Jesus shares our suffering;
He nurses us and heals us by His own wounds and stripes.
As we go through our valleys, He keeps us constant company.
And that is what makes the difference.
His presence is joy.

COLLEEN TOWNSEND EVANS

A SIMPLE TRUTH

Brokenness shapes character and prepares us to serve effectively.

WORDS TO REMEMBER

"Discipline...produces a harvest of righteousness and peace." — Hebrews 12:11

AN UNDYING MYTH

A persistent myth circulates among spiritually attuned people. It claims if we follow God's purpose and vision for us, we'll always wind up living happily ever after. No pain or disappointment, no second-guessing ourselves and our ambiguous destinations. Just smooth sailing toward the afterlife.

This myth persists because we want to believe it. We reason, "If God is good and perfect, can't he provide us with the good life? Doesn't he want to?"

The answer on both counts is yes. He provided this perfect life in the Garden of Eden, but we foiled the plan. Because of our choice to sin, even redeemed humanity can't know perfection until we reach heaven, but the essence of an unencumbered existence haunts our spiritual memory. We sense that somewhere perfection was possible, and we live with the desire but not the capability to acquire seamless lives.

Despite our wishes, Jesus said in the world we will experience tribulation (John 16:33), and this trouble arrives in many forms. Christians encounter divorce, illness, job loss, bankruptcy, the death of loved ones, public humiliation, and every trial known to humanity. We can blithely say, "Everything happens for a reason," but at times a justifiable cause is as impossible to grasp as the smoke of our cindered lives.

FIRST THOUGHTS

1. What are your candid feelings about God's children experiencing pain?

2. Is there a trial in your life that you don't understand? If so, briefly describe it.

3. If your answer to #2 is yes, what are your requests to God regarding this trial? How has he responded to them?

THE GOD OF ALL COMFORT

God grieves with us and cares deeply about our broken hearts. Often he does not eradicate a difficulty — at least not immediately — but abides with us through it, whether or not we sense his presence. He longs to comfort and heal us, turning our ashes into beauty, our mourning into joy, our weakness into praise.

4. What do these verses say about God's presence and participation in trials?
  • Deuteronomy 31:6*

- Matthew 28:20

- John 14:16—17*

- 2 Corinthians 1:3—4*

5. According to these verses, how does God comfort us?
  - Psalm 94:17—19*

  - Psalm 119:49—52*

  - Isaiah 40:1 (These words were spoken to the prophet Isaiah.)

  - John 16:33

  - Romans 15:4

  - 1 Thessalonians 5:11*

6. Have you felt God's comfort during times of brokenness? Why, or why not?

7. In addition to comforting and abiding with us, God wants to use the pain to make us more holy, pliable, credible, and compassionate as we fulfill our purpose. During trials, what transformations does he perform?

- Galatians 5:22—25*

- Philippians 2:1—8*

- Philippians 2:14—16

- Philippians 4:11—12*

- Colossians 1:10—12*

- 1 Peter 4:10

8. Knowing that God uses our trials to develop character, how can we respond to pain? See James 1:2–4* and Romans 12:12, 14, 17–21*. When we respond this way, what are the results?

9. Read Proverbs 14:10–14*. What happens when we resist God's character-building process?

T R A V E L I N G T H E W A S T E L A N D

To the unholy mind suffering squanders talent, but to be spiritually useful to God we must periodically waste ourselves in the valley of brokenness. In this valley God tenderly picks up our shattered pieces and remolds them into the image of his son.

10. In Isaiah 42:3*, what does God promise about his redesign process?

11. In the Old Testament God's people presented drink offerings of oil and wine along with various sacrifices for entering into fellowship

with God or for purifying themselves from sin. To pour out an expensive wine before the Lord was a holy task; what appeared to man as a "waste" of a fine product was an act of consecration to God.

We, too, can be drink offerings to the Lord. At times it can feel as though God is wasting our time and talents. What was Paul's attitude toward his life being "wasted" in God's service?

• Philippians 2:17*

• 2 Timothy 4:6–7

12. Pain prepares us to use our valuable talents in humble service, wiping feet with the sweet aroma of our abilities. When we suffer, we grow willing to give up our rights for God's desires and to serve with reverence instead of selfish ambition.

Through your purpose, how might God be asking you to humbly serve others?

REAPING THE REWARDS

When passing through painful times, it's difficult to imagine a reward on the other side. But God promises he'll work out our circumstances for good. Romans 8:28 says, "And we know that in all things God works for the good of those who love him, who have been called according to his purpose."

Often when we look back, we're granted the honor of seeing the good that God created. But sometimes it's hard to discern. We do not fully comprehend the results in our lifetime. The Bible presents examples of both.

13. Read about the suffering of Joseph (Genesis 37:12—45:13) and Job (Job 1:5—2:10; 42:10—17*). For each story, answer these questions:
- What was the nature and extent of the suffering?
- At the time did God reveal a reason for the difficulty?
- How did the struggling person respond to the trial?
- How did pain shape the person's character?
- How did the difficulty affect those associated with this person?
- What was the eventual outcome of the suffering?
- What can you learn from this person's life?

JOSEPH   JOB

UPROOTING BESETTING SINS

Suffering doesn't just result from circumstances beyond our control; we also feel pain from our sin, and perhaps this is the deepest grief of all. Sometimes it's easier to manage external difficulties than internal failings and personal transgressions. When we sin, we can't pass the guilt to anyone else; the blame falls on us.

Sin compromises our relationship with God and the full pursuit of purpose. These aren't the assorted daily sins we confess and throw away, although it's important to cleanse ourselves from these. These are the besetting sins, the repeated transgressions we can't release — the gnawing wrongdoings that trouble and isolate us. God wants to use this pain to change us, too.

God whispers to us in our pleasures, speaks in our con-science, and shouts in our pains. It is His megaphone to rouse a deaf world. — C. S. Lewis

14. How do these sins break us? See Psalm 38:1—14*.

15. According to Hebrews 2:14—18*, how has Jesus already responded to our brokenness from sin?

16. What personal sins could be breaking you? Describe their effects.

17. What can you do with this brokenness? See Psalm 38:15–22*.

IN PRAISE OF WEAKNESS

When we risk the pursuit of purpose, we'll eventually bump against overwhelming situations that expose how weak we really are. We feel bereft and inadequate, and contrary to our culture's demands, *this is precisely how God wants us to feel* so we'll depend on him. When we finally grasp this concept, it's a relief to drop our facade of rugged individualism, admit that we're weak, and allow him to guide and strengthen us.

18. Paul pushed this concept further by suggesting that we delight in our weaknesses. When he petitioned God to remove his "thorn in the flesh," the Lord replied, "My grace is sufficient for you, for my power is made perfect in weakness." What was Paul's response (2 Corinthians 12:7–10*)?

19. How else does God assure us that he can use our weaknesses?
   • Acts 17:24—28

   • 1 Corinthians 1:26—31*

   • 2 Corinthians 3:4—6*

CONFESSING INADEQUACY

God specializes in taking the "weaklings" of the world and turning them into strong and beautiful souls. In his eyes brokenness is not a failure; it is the gateway to a deeper spirituality. When we confess our inadequacy, we give God the opportunity to express his graciousness to and through us.

20. What weaknesses and inadequacies do you offer to God? Write out a prayer that offers these "downfalls" to God and asks for his strength.
   Dear God,

   Amen.

A PEACEABLE HARVEST

Like us, Jesus Christ suffered pain and temptation while on the earth. Christ's purpose was to seek and save the lost, and to accomplish this mission he accepted a horrible death by crucifixion. On the cross he bore the punishment for our sins, so when we accept his gift of blood-stained salvation, we exchange eternal damnation for everlasting life.

The prophet Isaiah poetically predicted Christ's suffering in Isaiah 53:3–5.

> *He was despised and rejected by men,*
> *a man of sorrows, and familiar with suffering.*
> *Like one from whom men hide their faces*
> *he was despised, and we esteemed him not.*
> *Surely he took up our infirmities*
> *and carried our sorrows,*
> *yet we considered him stricken by God,*
> *smitten by him, and afflicted.*
> *But he was pierced for our transgressions,*
> *he was crushed for our iniquities;*
> *the punishment that brought us peace was upon him,*
> *and by his wounds we are healed.*

21. In the preceding passage, circle the ways Christ suffered for us. What rewards do we receive from Christ's suffering? Underline them.

OUR RESPONSE

Christ agonized on the cross to redeem our eternity but also to bring a peace that passes all understanding and a purity of heart while traveling this planet. God is good and wants to impart his goodness to us. By his wounds we are healed.

22. What response would you like to have toward Christ's suffering for us? How can you cultivate this response?

23. What major principle do you want to remember from this session? Why?

OPTIONAL ACTIVITIES

1. Read chapter six, "Brokenness," in the book *Designing a Woman's Life*.

2. Gather a group of close friends who have experienced trials and ask each person to tell her "brokenness" story in a few minutes. Create a list of all the changes for the good that God accomplished in each individual. Celebrate the changes.

3. Write encouraging notes to friends and acquaintances who are in pain. Comfort them and share how God has worked in your life through brokenness.

4. Make a list of the qualities you'd like God to develop in you while traveling the wasteland of brokenness. Commit the list to him and tuck it away for review at a later date.

5. Write out a prayer of forgiveness. Forgive the people who have caused you pain. Forgive God for allowing the pain. Forgive yourself for how you've behaved through difficulty.

6. In addition to Joseph and Job, study other biblical people who passed through pain, answering the questions in #13 of the study session.

Next Session: Explore how to persevere toward your goal.

Perseverance

Plodding Ahead with Heart and Hope

❧

What then should we be?
That each will answer for himself.
But for myself and to myself I say:
Though stripped of every armor, be a warrior —
a warrior of the spirit, for what the spirit knows.

DOROTHY THOMPSON

A Simple Truth

To fulfill our purpose God calls us to persevere, regardless of the rewards.

Words to Remember

"We consider blessed those who have persevered." — James 5:11a

Independent of the Results

Midst rotted chicken pieces and soiled diapers, the poorest of the poor who live in one of Guatemala City's garbage dumps scavenge for scraps to eat. Into this decaying world stride Gladys and Lisbeth, two Guatemalan women who traded their comfortable counseling careers for a spiritual outreach to the "dump people."

"A lot of my friends thought I was crazy," remembers Gladys. "For a few years we didn't have any volunteers. I tried recruiting young people from my church, but a brother in the church told them not to help because of the danger. Others thought we'd catch a disease. People thought it was a phase and we'd get over it."

But Gladys and Lisbeth didn't get over it. Instead, they forged ahead, and the ministry burgeoned. It's often depressing and discouraging, but it's what they feel compelled to do and where they want to be. Both Gladys and Lisbeth receive invitations to teach or work with other ministries, but their hearts stay buried in the dump. These women can't envision their lives away from the *Casa del Alfarero's* needy landfill residents, and they dream about the people's future.

"I ask the Lord to not let me die until I see spiritual revival here," says Lisbeth. "We've been planting seeds for several years, and I would like to see the [people] seek the Lord sincerely. That is my desire, to see a spiritual revival here, because I know that's the exit to their pain and suffering. When we don't see changes, we still must maintain obedience to God. The Lord calls us to plant and bless, independently of the results."[1]

FIRST THOUGHTS

1. To you, what does it mean to persevere?

2. Describe a situation in which you persevered and received the desired results. How did you feel?

A CASE FOR ENDURANCE

Gladys and Lisbeth know how to persevere. They understand that God asks us to endure the delays and difficulties, sacrifices and celebrations, of a life purpose.

3. Why do we persevere? Look up these verses to explore some biblical reasons and rewards.

SCRIPTURE   REASON TO PERSEVERE
- Colossians 1:10–11*

SCRIPTURE	REASON TO PERSEVERE
• Hebrews 12:7*	
• James 1:12a	
• James 1:2–4*	
• James 5:11*	
• 1 Timothy 4:12, 15–16	
• 2 Timothy 2:3	
• 2 Timothy 2:10*	

4. Before embarking on our purpose, it helps to list the reasons for persevering so when hardship hits we can remind ourselves why we're not giving up. Review the reasons for endurance in #3. Which ones relate the most to your pursuit of purpose? Explain.

THE ULTIMATE REASON

A reason that underscores all of our justifications for perseverance is that God asks us to obey him. As we observed in a previous lesson, he considers obedience better than sacrifice (1 Samuel 15:22) and wants us to pursue purpose his way instead of ours.

5. Why can we trust God with our journey, whatever the outcome?
   • Jeremiah 29:11–13*

   • Proverbs 16:9

   • Jeremiah 17:7–8*

6. On the other hand, what does God say about his plans versus our plans, his outcomes compared to our hoped-for results?
   • Proverbs 20:24

   • Isaiah 55:8–9*

   • Jeremiah 10:23*

7. How can you learn to trust God's plans and outcomes more? After looking up these verses, add your own ideas to the list.
   • Psalm 77:10–12*

• Mark 9:23–24

• Romans 10:17*

• Others:

STARTING WITH COMMITMENT

When God places a purpose and vision within us, we'll accomplish nothing of spiritual significance by dabbling. From the beginning, we need to commit.

Purpose constitutes a voluntary vow to God, a sacred agreement not entered into lightly. Moses warned the Israelites about the sacredness of a vow to God. This is wise advice for us, too — not to discourage us from proclaiming our purpose, but to consecrate it.

8. What did Moses say in Deuteronomy 23:23?

9. What does the Bible say about our commitment and God's plans?
   • Psalm 37:5–7*

• Proverbs 16:3–4*

• 1 Peter 4:19

10. According to the verses in #9, what can you depend on if you commit your purpose and plans to the Lord?

FEELING NO FEAR

Whatever our purpose, we shouldn't let the idea of consecration paralyze us, making us reluctant to commit for fear we'll choose the wrong direction. Fearing mistakes overlooks the understanding, forgiving, revitalizing nature of God. He discerns between sincere misguidance and indifferent disobedience.

One does not discover new lands without consenting to lose sight of the shore for a very long time. — André Gide

11. How could you show God that you've committed your purpose and plans to him?

WRAPPED IN DELIGHT

Since I've known my friend Nancy she's firmly pursued her destiny as a pianist, although she's talented in several ways. She's sacrificed time, money, involvements, and childbearing for the joy of music, practicing hour upon hour to sensitively interpret a composer's work. She imparts this devotion to her piano students, and when she performs a concert, the single-mindedness pays off. Each time I hear Nancy play, I am awestruck.

Nancy doesn't persevere at the piano because she's forced to or mired in workaholism. She plays for the sheer love of it. If she quit the lessons with her master teacher, if a student never entered her studio, if the concert schedule dried up, she'd still play. Nancy is wrapped in the *delight* and *process* of her purpose, and pursuing any other mission would be unthinkable.

True perseverance springs from within, propelling us through peaks and valleys, joy and despair. It plods ahead with heart and hope, no matter what we see or how we feel. It is born from love.

12. According to these verses, how can we infuse our purpose with joy and delight? Can you think of other ways than those represented by the following verses?
   • Psalm 16:11*

   • Psalm 35:9

   • Psalm 37:4

- Psalm 40:8*

- Psalm 119:16*

- Other ways:

13. What do (or will) you enjoy about the *process* — the day by day doing — of pursuing your purpose? How can you focus more on the process than the end results?

PILING UP STONES

Even if we delight in the process of our purpose, sometimes persevering feels like traveling blindfolded. Before we step forward, it's good to look back at God's past trustworthiness for encouragement and motivation. To help us remember, we can build memorials to significant expressions of God's constancy.

14. In Joshua 3—4, Joshua led the Israelites across the Jordan River into the promised land, and God wanted his people to remember

they had crossed on dry ground. In Joshua 4:1–5*, what does God instruct Joshua and the Israelites to do?

15. According to Joshua 4:6–8, 24*, what did the stones represent?

16. As you pursue your purpose, what memorials can you build to God's faithfulness during both the good and bad times?

SOWING AND REAPING

God wants us to harbor a wild hope when we sow the seeds of our purpose. Through years of preparation, through times of inconsistent or nonexistent results, he asks that we persevere for the joy of our purpose and love for him.

> *It takes so much to be a full human being*
> *that there are very few who have the courage*
> *to pay the price. — Morris L. West*

God desires that, like natural-born gardeners, we find satisfaction in the *process* of our purpose — obeying, serving, growing — and leave the outcome to him. He may even test our perseverance when we see no results or rewards.

17. Sometimes we reap what we sow; sometimes we don't. Read the parable of the sower and Jesus' interpretation of it in Matthew 13:1—8, 18—23*. When we sow the seeds of our purpose, what are the varied spiritual results in people's lives?

18. In the parable, what was the sower's role, whether or not the seeds sprouted? How does this apply to you?

19. Read Jesus' teaching about sowing and reaping in John 4:34—38*. What is the relationship between the spiritual sower and the reaper?

20. Sometimes we're the sower. Other times we're the reaper. How might you become willing to fulfill either of these roles as God desires?

21. The Book of Hebrews tells about people who persevered and lived by faith but didn't receive the rewards they'd hoped for. Read about these people in Hebrews 11 and then answer these questions:
   • What is the meaning of faith (verse 1*)?

   • What was the end result of these people's pursuit of purpose and obedience to God (verse 13*)?

   • What attitude did these persevering people have in common (verses 13—16*)?

   • What was God's response to these people (verse 16*)?

• What good plan did God have in mind that these people could not see while on the earth (verses 39–40*)?

22. In Hebrews 12:1–4*, what reasons does Paul give for our perseverance?

23. What main idea do you want to remember from this session about perseverance?

OPTIONAL ACTIVITIES

1. Read chapter seven, "Perseverance," in *Designing a Woman's Life*.

2. Create an act of consecration to dedicate your purpose to God. You could write a mission statement in a journal or hold a private dedication service with a friend. You might inscribe a motivational scripture on a plaque or write a letter of commitment and read it aloud to God. Your family could celebrate with a special meal or activity. Or your study group could devote time to commissioning prayer.

Whatever you do, an act of consecration works best when it combines *writing* out a purpose and *verbalizing* it to at least one person.

3. Designate a friend who will encourage you and hold you accountable for persevering when times get tough.

4. Read the Old Testament stories of the people mentioned in Hebrews 11. What can you learn about perseverance from them?

5. Count your blessings. List the good things you've received when you've persevered.

6. Read about the lives of Amy Carmichael and Corrie ten Boom. How did these women persevere, no matter the circumstances? What were their rewards? What can you learn from them?

Next Session: Study how you can influence others with your purpose.

Session Eight

Influence

Reaching Out to Make a Difference

❧

Everyone reaches, but not everyone touches.
Reaching is instinctive;
but for the most part touching is learned.
In touching we give and receive, talk and listen,
share ourselves and see into another.
And not everyone can do that or will do it.

GAIL MACDONALD

A SIMPLE TRUTH

Through our purpose we can influence the world for God's kingdom.

WORDS TO REMEMBER

"'You are my witnesses,' declares the LORD, 'and my servant whom I have chosen.'" — Isaiah 43:10a

A LOT TO LEARN

In one of my first "official" positions of influence I stumbled into a conflict I'll never forget. Around age sixteen I wrote and directed a play produced by my church's youth group, and on the Saturday before a Sunday evening performance for our small congregation, the thespians among us met at church for an overdue rehearsal.

Despite our eleventh-hour gathering the rehearsal progressed smoothly, until I decided the play would fare better if we performed in the basement instead of the sanctuary. (I've forgotten the reason I considered this a clever idea.) Not many agreed, but I thought being their leader meant we did things my way. So cast members begrudgingly hauled the homespun props downstairs, including a couch that barely passed through a narrow stairwell.

Within minutes after carting everything downstairs I figured the basement wasn't the right place after all. (I've always needed to see furniture arranged before I settle on it.) *Okay, let's move things back upstairs,* I decided. It made sense to me, but articulating my decision instigated a fallout. The guys felt especially annoyed because they'd carried the heavy pieces.

The final blow occurred when halfway up the stairs the couch got stuck on the railings. *Really stuck.* The guys and I lost our patience, exchanged blaming words, and stood on each side of the lodged couch, glowering at each other.

I had a lot to learn about influence.

FIRST THOUGHTS

1. What is the meaning of influence? Without looking through this session, write out your definition.

2. Describe someone who has influenced you positively. As you fulfill your purpose, how would you like to model after her or him?

THE PRIVILEGE OF SERVANTHOOD

After experiencing brokenness and persevering in our purpose, God blesses us with the privilege of spiritual influence. But contrary to my sixteen-year-old logic, *influence isn't about power and getting what we want. It's about servanthood and giving our best to others,* whatever our position in life.

This is another principle of Christ's kingdom that's difficult for our control-oriented culture to grasp. We're encouraged to scramble to the top, revel in the perks, and look down on the "little people" below. But Christ taught his followers to influence through servanthood and humility.

The world cannot always understand one's profession of faith, but it can understand service. — Ian Maclaren

3. What did Christ teach in Matthew 10:38—39* and Mark 9:33—35* about finding our place of service? What do you think he meant by this instruction?

4. Because our culture's advice is to "rise to the top," we can feel reluctant to serve. Do you believe any of the following statements? If so, circle them.

- To serve, I must forsake everything I desire to do in life.
- Servanthood means I'm always a follower, never a leader.
- If I serve, people will think I'm "wimpy."
- Servants never get noticed for what they do.
- Servants can't feel gratified in their role.
- People don't respect servants.
- Servants are passive, not assertive or initiators.

5. All of the above statements are false. In contrast, what do these scriptures teach about serving and servanthood?

- Matthew 4:10*

- Matthew 6:24

- John 12:26*

• John 13:15—17

• Romans 7:6

• Romans 14:17—18*

• Galatians 5:13*

6. Based on what you learned in #5, summarize the biblical approach to servanthood.

7. Read in Mark 10:45* and Philippians 2:6—8* how Christ modeled servanthood. What were the characteristics of his servanthood toward us?

8. How can you model biblical, Christlike servanthood as you fulfill your purpose?

HAND IN HAND WITH HUMILITY

Servanthood and humility walk hand in hand. However, humility does not mean we think poorly of ourselves, but rather through God's grace we think "rightly" about ourselves. That is, we are sinners saved through Jesus Christ's sacrifice on the cross and are valuable to him and his service.

> *Nothing sets a person so much out of the devil's reach as humility.* — Jonathan Edwards

In 1 Timothy 1:15–16 Paul explained, "Here is a trustworthy saying that deserves full acceptance: Christ Jesus came into the world to save sinners — of whom I am the worst. But for that very reason I was shown mercy so that in me, the worst of sinners, Christ Jesus might display his unlimited patience as an example for those who would believe on him and receive eternal life."

9. What do these verses tell us about humility?
  • Proverbs 15:33

  • Proverbs 16:19

  • Proverbs 22:4

  • Proverbs 29:23*

- Luke 14:11

- Colossians 3:12

- James 4:6, 10*

- 1 Peter 5:5—6

10. According to the verses in #9, what are the sacrifices and rewards of humility? How do you feel about these sacrifices and rewards?

SACRIFICES   REWARDS

THE CHARACTER OF INFLUENCE

When we spiritually influence others through our purpose, it is our character that ultimately touches people, not just our words, talents, or actions. So as we develop our purpose-related skills and plans, we need also to place a high priority on becoming more like Jesus.

11. See Galatians 5:22−23*. As we influence others through our purpose, what nine character qualities can the Holy Spirit express
through us? List them in the left column on the following page.
How can you express each of these qualities, or fruit of the Spirit,
while fulfilling your purpose? Jot your ideas in the right column.

QUALITIES   EXPRESSIONS

•

•

•

•

•

•

•

•

•

12. In many ways influencing others parallels leading them, even if we
aren't gifted as a leader or serve in an "up-front" capacity in the

Body of Christ. According to these passages, how does a leader or influencer behave?

- 1 Timothy 3:1—13

- Titus 2:1—10*

- 1 Peter 5:1—3

13. Of these behaviors, which three would be most important for fulfilling your purpose? Why?

14. The letters of 1 and 2 Peter discuss how Christ's followers should conduct themselves in the world. As we seek to influence, how can we behave?

- 1 Peter 1:22; 2:1—2

- 1 Peter 2:11—20*

- 1 Peter 3:8—17

- 1 Peter 4:7—11*

- 2 Peter 1:5—10*

- 2 Peter 3:14

LOVING ONE ANOTHER

A few blocks from my home an old barnyard sits on the edge of a business district, a stubborn survivor of the city's steady sprawl. I've wondered how many accidents this slice of country life causes as it sits (and smells) unexpectedly at a busy intersection between commercial and residential neighborhoods. But it's not the rural ambiance that distracts motorists; it's the proverbs the owner paints on a side of an old barn facing the north and west traffic.

Twenty-three years ago the owner recovered from a life-threatening brain tumor and told her children, "I feel well enough for a party, and you can even paint the barn." So that's what the family did, and almost every year a new, thought-provoking quotation appears on the barn's backside. The current slogan proclaims, "What humanity is is you being you and me being me and no add ons."[1]

This proverb invites me to think about my expectations toward the people in my life. I know I'm not to condone sin, but for the most part, do I let them be themselves, with no add ons? Or do I expect them to be like me? Do I respect their purposes in life or that they may feel no destiny at all?

15. How would you answer the previous questions?

16. During his ministry on earth, Jesus emphasized that his followers should love one another. Kneeling in a garden before his arrest and crucifixion he prayed we would all be one. Read John 17:11, 20—23* and summarize the Lord's requests about the spiritual family's "oneness."

17. Why would Jesus believe loving one another to be so important?

18. Contrary to what we're prone to think and insist upon, "oneness" is not every Christian thinking and living exactly the same way. It involves how we treat one another. According to Ephesians 4:20—5:1*, how are we to relate to our spiritual brothers and sisters?

19. How could loving spiritual sisters and brothers affect your pursuit of purpose?

CELEBRATING OUR PURPOSE

One way to express this love centers on celebrating our diverse life purposes and the God-inspired visions and personal choices that flow from individual destinies.

20. Think of the women you're associated with regularly. How can you respect and support their purposes in life?

21. What one idea do you want to remember from this session about influence?

OPTIONAL ACTIVITIES

1. Read chapter eight, "Influence," in the book *Designing a Woman's Life*.

2. In the *Designing* book, review the section on "Risking Vulnerability" (page 140). How can you be vulnerable with the recipients of your purpose?

3. In the *Designing* book, consider the section on "Questing for Quality" (page 142). How can you build quality into the fulfillment of your purpose?

4. Interview women who are influencers. What qualities do they feel are important for making an impact on others?

5. Create a list of the most important qualities you want to develop in relationship to your purpose. Place the list in your Bible, use it as a prayer reminder, and periodically review it to check your progress.

6. Make a list of the main points you want to remember from this entire study (eight sessions). Post it where you'll see it every day.

7. Create Scripture memory cards based on the "Words to Remember" verses from each lesson. Encourage yourself with them in the coming months.

Exploration

More Books about Purposeful Living

Although not all of these books support a Christian viewpoint, they present assorted truths about the topics covered in the *Designing a Woman's Life* book and Bible study. Read with discernment, these titles can enhance the search for purpose.

Bolles, Richard N. *How to Find Your Mission in Life*. Berkeley: Ten Speed Press, 1991.

Couchman, Judith. *Designing a Woman's Life*. Sisters, Ore.: Multnomah, 1995.

Covey, Stephen. *The Seven Habits of Highly Effective People*. New York: Simon and Schuster, 1989.

Heald, Cynthia. *Becoming a Woman of Purpose*. Colorado Springs: NavPress, 1994.

McCarthy, Kevin. *The On-Purpose Person*. Colorado Springs: Piñon Press, 1992.

Myers, Warren and Ruth. *Discovering God's Will*. Colorado Springs: NavPress, 1980.

Potter, Beverly. *Finding a Path with a Heart: How to Go from Burnout to Bliss*. Ronin Publishing, 1995.

Sheehy, Gail. *New Passages: Mapping Your Life Across Time.* New York: Random House, 1995.

Sher, Barbara. *I Could Do Anything If I Only Knew What It Was.* New York: Delacorte Press, 1994.

Sinetar, Marsha. *Do What You Love, the Money Will Follow.* New York: Dell Publishing, 1987.

Sinetar, Marsha. *To Build the Life You Want, Create the Work You Love.* New York: St. Martin's Press, 1995.

Stephen, Naomi. *Fulfill Your Soul's Purpose: Ten Creative Paths to Your Life Mission.* Walpole, N.H.: Stillpoint Publishing, 1994.

Stoddard, Alexandra. *Making Choices: Discover the Joy of Living the Life You Want to Lead.* New York: Avon Books, 1994.

Tieger, Paul and Barbara Barron-Tieger. *Do What You Are: Discover the Perfect Career for You through the Secret of Personality Type.* Boston: Little, Brown and Company, 1992.

Viscott, David. *Risking.* New York: Pocket Books, 1977.

Introduction

   1. Søren Kierkegaard, quoted in John Bartlett, *Familiar Quotations* (Boston: Little, Brown and Company, 1980), 552.

Session Two

   1. *Webster's New World Dictionary*, 2d college ed., s.v. "purpose."

   2. Diagram adapted from *How to Find Your Mission in Life* by Richard Bolles.

   3. The Presbyterian Church in America, *The Confession of Faith*, 2d ed. (Atlanta: Committee for Christian Education and Publications, 1986).

Session Three

   1. Hannah Whitall Smith, *Daily Devotions from the Christian's Secret of a Happy Life* (Old Tappan, N.J.: Fleming H. Revell Company, 1985), 87.

   2. *Chariots of Fire*, prod. David Puttnam, 124 min., Warner Home Video, 1982, videocassette.

   3. Richard Nelson Bolles, *How to Find Your Mission in Life* (Berkeley: Ten Speed Press, 1991), 43.

   4. Frederick Buechner, *Wishful Thinking: A Theological ABC* (New York: Harper and Row, Publishers, 1973), 95.

   5. Marsha Sinetar, *To Build the Life You Want, Create the Work You Love* (New York: St. Martin's Press, 1995), 47.

Session Four

   1. John Bartlett, *Familiar Quotations* (Boston: Little, Brown and Company, 1980), 520.

2. Carly Simon, "The Stuff That Dreams Are Made Of" on *Coming Around Again*, Arista, audiocassette.

Session Five

1. Ralph G. Martin, *Henry and Clare: An Intimate Portrait of the Luces* (New York: G. P. Putnam's Sons, 1991), 408.

2. Ann Spangler, ed., *Bright Legacy: Portraits of Ten Outstanding Christian Women* (Ann Arbor, Mich.: Servant Books, 1983), 124-49.

3. *Webster's New World Dictionary*, s.v. "focus."

4. Anne Wilson Schaef, *Meditations for Women Who Do Too Much* (San Francisco: HarperSanFrancisco, 1990), March 29 entry.

5. Craig Nakken, *The Addictive Personality: Roots, Rituals, Recovery* (Minneapolis: Hazelden, 1988), 21–23.

6. Martha Thatcher, *The Freedom of Obedience* (Colorado Springs: NavPress, 1986), 110.

Session Seven

1. Ana Gascon Ivey, "Down in the Dumps in Guatemala," *Clarity*, July/August 1994. Used by permission.

Session Eight

1. "Twenty-three years of barnyard wisdom," *Colorado Springs Gazette Telegraph*, 6 July 1995.